ENGLISH CATHEDRALS

JOHN CURTIS

Text by Richard Ashby

SALMON

INTRODUCTION

A 'cathedra' is the seat or chair of a Bishop, the symbol of his office as teacher, preacher and chief pastor of the geographical area or 'diocese' which is in his care. A cathedral is the building which contains the 'cathedra'. While no cathedrals survive from the earliest Christian period in England, their Norman successors, often altered, rebuilt, extended and completed by later generations, are the greatest public buildings of their time. Early dioceses were very large and at the Reformation, Henry VIII created new ones whose cathedrals were formerly great abbey churches. Further dioceses were created in the 19th and 20th centuries and more churches were designated cathedrals, often with much rebuilding and enlargement following.

Norwich Cathedral with its 'cathedra'

These beautiful buildings exhibit the development of architectural styles from the heaviest Romanesque of the early Norman period to the walls of light stone and glass which characterise the Perpendicular. The late Victorian and early 20th century cathedrals look back to these earlier styles. Over the centuries cathedrals have suffered the ravages of time, neglect, war and restoration. In spite of the general decline in religious practice in this country, cathedrals are more visited and used than at any other period in their history. They are loved and cared for as never before and today, we can see them in probably a better condition than at any time since they were built.

DURHAM CATHEDRAL

The seat of the Prince-Bishops of Durham is suitably imposing. It is set high above the River Wear where it dominates the skyline and the approach to the city by both rail and road. This fine Norman building contains the tombs of the Venerable Bede, the father of English learning, and holy St Cuthbert, the Prior of Lindisfarne, whose remains were brought here when the monks had to abandon their island in the face of invasion from the north.

CHESTER CATHEDRAL

Originally a great Benedictine abbey, on its dissolution by Henry VIII, Chester became a cathedral in 1540. Unusually, not only the great church but also many of its surrounding buildings were preserved so that the visitor can see how an English abbey would have looked before the Reformation swept so much away.

PETERBOROUGH CATHEDRAL

One of the great cathedrals of eastern England, Peterborough is the final resting place of Catherine of Aragon, Henry VIII's first wife, whose divorce by the King led to the breach with the Catholic Church and the creation of the Church of England. Mary Queen of Scots, executed by Henry's daughter Elizabeth, was also first buried here, although she now lies in Westminster Abbey.

HEREFORD CATHEDRAL

The Norman cathedral at Hereford stands above the bridge over the River Wye as if on guard, as indeed it has been for over a thousand years. This part of England, bordering Wales, was quite lawless when the diocese was founded in the 7th century. When the Normans came to pacify the area their new military defences enclosed the cathedral which they immediately started to rebuild. It has two magnificent treasures. The first is the most extensive remaining medieval library of some fifteen hundred chained books. Here also is the 13th century 'Mappa Mundi', a unique pictorial map of the world as it was then known, with the Holy Land and Jerusalem at its centre.

LINCOLN CATHEDRAL

Lincoln Cathedral crowns the hill from which much of its stone was quarried and its three towers are visible from miles around. It faces the walls of the Norman castle, and the original Norman cathedral was destroyed by an earthquake in 1185. Only the west front remained standing and even that was much altered in the subsequent rebuilding. So Lincoln, like Wells, is built in the 'Early English' Gothic style, with soaring columns of local limestone and Purbeck marble. Amongst the wealth of carvings, including angels playing their instruments in the great Angel Choir, is the famous 'Lincoln Imp' who looks out into the church from high up behind the high altar. In a small side chapel dedicated to St Blaise, the Patron Saint of Wool Combers, are lovely murals by the 'Bloomsbury Group' painter, Duncan Grant.

RIPON CATHEDRAL

Ripon became a cathedral in 1836, before which it was a 'Collegiate Church', that is a parish church served by a 'College' of priests, one of a number of such mother churches in the very large diocese of York. It stands on a site which has been used for Christian worship since the 7th century and St Wilfrid's Saxon crypt still survives under the later building.

GLOUCESTER CATHEDRAL

A Saxon abbey was founded here in 681. It was in the third monastery on this site that William the Conqueror gave the order for the compilation of the Domesday Book in 1085. Henry III was crowned here in 1216 at the age of nine and Edward II was buried here following his foul murder at Berkeley Castle. More recently parts of the cathedral were used for the filming of the *Harry Potter* books.

YORK MINSTER

York Minster is the second great church in English Christendom, the seat of one of England's two Archbishops and the greatest of all the medieval Gothic cathedrals. Inside it is possible to see the whole course of the development of English Gothic architecture from Early English to Perpendicular. It has the finest collection of medieval stained glass remaining in the country.

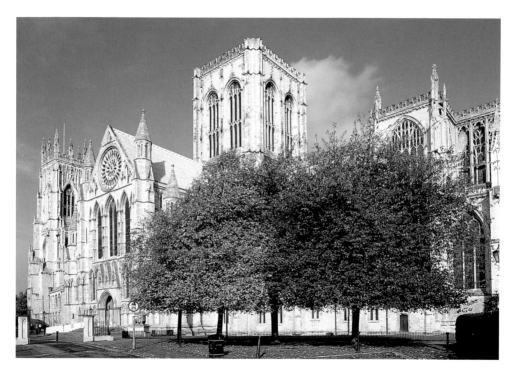

BRISTOL CATHEDRAL

Bristol Cathedral is the only medieval 'hall-church' cathedral in the country, where the roof of the nave and aisles all reach to the same height; it was the first of this type in the whole of Europe. Rebuilding was halted by the turmoil of the Reformation, and the nave and the two western towers were not completed until the 19th century. The cathedral is also unique in having two Lady Chapels and has a wonderful Norman chapter house.

SOUTHWARK CATHEDRAL

London's second cathedral is tucked away on the South Bank of the Thames hemmed in by railway lines, warehouses and a lively market. It dates from the 13th century and is London's oldest Gothic building. In preparation for the creation of the diocese of Southwark a major rebuilding took place and it became a cathedral in 1905.

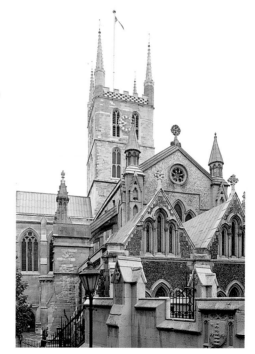

CANTERBURY CATHEDRAL

Canterbury is the cradle of English Christianity. In a famous legend Pope Gregory is said to have seen beautiful fair-haired children being sold as slaves in the market in Rome. On being told where they came from he replied 'Not Angles (English) but angels'. The Pope thus ordered St Augustine and his monks to England to preach Christianity to the pagan inhabitants and they were granted a base at Canterbury from which to begin their work of conversion by the king of Kent. Canterbury has therefore always been a special place of pilgrimage. It became even more famous when Archbishop Thomas à Becket was murdered here during the reign of Henry II and his shrine drew pilgrims from far and wide. Although the shrine was destroyed during the Reformation pilgrims still come, amongst them Pope John Paul II who met the Archbishop of Canterbury here in 1982.

CARLISLE CATHEDRAL

History has not been kind to the border country which was fought over by the English and Scots for centuries during which Carlisle and its cathedral often suffered badly. In the English Civil War the Puritans demolished most of the nave and used the stones to fortify the city against the Royalists. It was never rebuilt and the result is the smallest of the English cathedrals.

CHICHESTER CATHEDRAL

Chichester is situated between the South Downs and the sea. Indeed, the spire is the only one of all of England's cathedrals to be visible from the sea. It is one of the smaller English cathedrals but the double aisles, formed out of a range of side chapels in the 13th century, give it a light spaciousness. In the mid 19th century the stone screen, or 'pulpitum', which separates the nave from the choir, was removed, precipitating a spectacular collapse of the spire which was finely reconstructed by the Victorians. The screen, which luckily had been stored and not destroyed, was reinstated in 1961. The cathedral is notable for its 20th century art with fine works by John Piper, Graham Sutherland and Marc Chagall. Outside is a unique medieval detached bell tower and a lovely 'close'.

ROCHESTER CATHEDRAL

Rochester was the second diocese founded by St Augustine and thus this lesser known cathedral has a history longer than any other with the exception of Canterbury. It stands in very close relation with the adjacent castle, symbolising those two pillars of Norman rule, church and state. Charles Dickens grew up nearby and his last unfinished novel, *The Mystery of Edwin Drood* is set here.

SOUTHWELL MINSTER

The cathedral for the Nottinghamshire area was originally, like Ripon, a mother church for this part of the large diocese of York. Southwell is England's smallest cathedral city and grew up around its fine Norman church. The 'Leaves of Southwell' are a profusion of magnificent carvings in and around the chapter house.

LICHFIELD CATHEDRAL

Lichfield was badly damaged in a siege during the English Civil War after which the Parliamentary soldiers stripped the lead from the cathedral roof and the walls were used as a quarry. Great restorations followed. The three graceful spires, which give the cathedral its unique silhouette, are known locally as 'The Ladies of the Vale'.

ST PAUL'S, LONDON CATHEDRAL

Si monumentum requiris, circumspice (If you seek his monument, look around you). So runs the inscription on the tomb of Sir Christopher Wren, the 17th century architect of this most famous of all English cathedrals. St Paul's is also the nation's church and has become the setting for important state occasions, such as royal weddings, state funerals and events of national thanksgiving.

ELY CATHEDRAL

The 'Cathedral of the Fens' has often been likened to a ship, an image which must have been even more powerful before the surrounding land was drained. Its glory is the lantern, an amazing achievement for the medieval engineers and architects. There is nothing like it in the whole of Europe.

EXETER CATHEDRAL

The original seat of the diocese covering Devon and Cornwall was at Crediton. In 1050 it was transferred to Exeter, which was a walled city and could thus be better defended. Of the original Norman cathedral only the two great towers remain, standing, unusually, on the north and south sides of the building. It was subsequently rebuilt and is an almost entirely 13th and 14th century cathedral built at the peak of the 'Decorated' Gothic architectural style. Like Canterbury, Exeter was the victim of one of the notorious Second World War 'Baedeker' raids on cities of no strategic importance and both city and cathedral were extensively damaged. The cathedral has since been finely restored.

WORCESTER CATHEDRAL

Above a bend of the River Severn and the Worcester County Cricket Ground, the setting of this cathedral is the epitome of Englishness. Sir Edward Elgar, England's finest composer, spent much of his life nearby and his music is indelibly linked with the cathedral, which contains a fine memorial window to him.

SALISBURY CATHEDRAL

The original centre of Christianity in this area was at Old Sarum, in origin an Iron Age fort on a chalk hill, about two miles away from its present site. Its inconvenience and uncomfortably exposed position led to the removal of the cathedral to its present site by the River Avon. It was begun in 1220 and, unlike all English cathedrals, except St Paul's in London, was completed, without a break, to its original design. Salisbury's particular claim to fame is its spire, the tallest in all England and the second highest in Europe. It was constructed around a wooden scaffolding which remains inside along with the wooden windlass which is still used. The weight of the spire placed such a strain on the tower and columns below and the inadequate foundations, that additional strainer arches had to be inserted to prevent its collapse.

ST ALBANS CATHEDRAL

St Alban, a young Roman citizen, was beheaded for his faith in 209 AD. The abbey, built on the site of his martyrdom, became the most important in England and provided the only English Pope in 1154. There is no stone hereabouts, so much of the great church is built of the bricks taken from the ruins of the Roman town of Verulamium. 13th century mural paintings survive in the nave.

WINCHESTER CATHEDRAL

Winchester was the capital of the Saxon
Kingdom of Wessex and here are the graves
of Alfred the Great and the Danish King
Canute and his wife. Alfred's teacher, the
holy Bishop Swithun would not be buried
inside the cathedral and when his remains
were moved inside, a century later, it is said
that it rained for the following forty days.

LIVERPOOL CATHEDRAL

Liverpool is the largest Anglican cathedral
in the world and twice the size of St Paul's
in London. It outdoes all others with the
highest arches, heaviest bells and largest
organ. Its architect, Giles Gilbert Scott, was
only 22 when his winning design was
selected from more than a hundred
competitors. Initially it was thought that
Scott was too young to undertake such an
enormous task on his own and so the design
for the Lady Chapel, which was built first,
was done in collaboration with the eminent
architect George Bodley. After Bodley died
Scott continued by himself. The foundation
stone was laid in 1904 and Scott worked on
his building until his death in 1960,
modifying his designs several times. The
cathedral was not finally completed until
1978. With the Roman Catholic Cathedral
it dominates the Liverpool skyline.

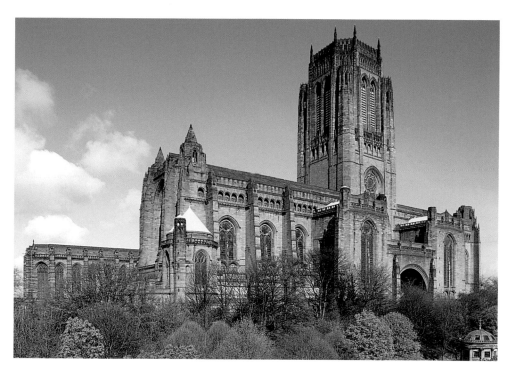

TRURO CATHEDRAL

The new diocese was created in 1877 and Truro Cathedral is the first of the 'modern' cathedrals. Here is an essay in French architecture set in a small Cornish town. It stands on the site of the town's ancient Parish Church, a Tudor aisle of which it incorporates. It was completed in 1910. The site is cramped, hemmed in by other buildings and the architect's skilful use of perspective makes it appear bigger inside than it really is. Outside, one might for a moment think one is in Brittany; the three tall spires dominate its surroundings. The famous service of Nine Lessons and Carols for Christmas Eve was devised by the first Bishop of Truro and first used in the temporary cathedral in 1880.

GUILDFORD CATHEDRAL

Guildford and Liverpool are the only two Anglican cathedrals built on entirely new sites since the Middle Ages. It stands in a commanding position on Stag Hill and its building, interrupted by the war, took 30 years. It is truly a 'people's church', being built of bricks, made from the hill itself, and bought by thousands of people in the diocese.

COVENTRY CATHEDRAL

Much of the city, including its ancient cathedral, was destroyed in the great air raid of 14th November 1940. The cathedral ruins were preserved and are linked to the new building consecrated in 1962. Coventry retains the traditional plan but uses striking contemporary art in glass, stone, wood, metal and tapestry. Outside, Sir Jacob Epstein's sculpture of St Michael overcoming the Devil symbolises the rebirth of both city and cathedral.

WELLS CATHEDRAL

Nestling beneath the Mendip Hills, Wells has been called the 'Queen of Cathedrals'. Its glory is the incomparable west front, an amazing display of medieval figure carving and one of the greatest of such sights in England. The cathedral is built of Doulting Stone, still quarried only a few miles away and in use for repair and restoration. It is notable for being the first medieval building in England to have pointed arches. The common problem of the tower being too heavy for its columns and foundations below has been elegantly solved by the insertion of the spectacular strainer arches, such a feature of the interior. Amongst the treasures are a chained library and a 14th century clock in the north transept with a 24 hour dial and horsemen who revolve when the clock strikes.

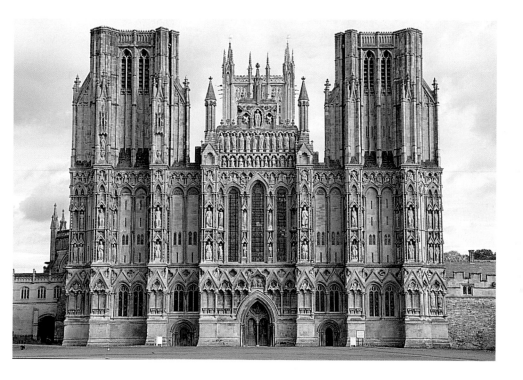

NORWICH CATHEDRAL

Once Norwich was the second city of the Kingdom, and its wealth is reflected in the magnificence of its cathedral which retains its original Norman ground plan. It has the second longest nave after Ely and the second highest spire after Salisbury. Alone amongst English cathedrals, it preserves an ancient bishop's chair, the 'cathedra', dating from Saxon times which is placed behind the High Altar in the early Christian manner.

Published in Great Britain by J. Salmon Ltd., Sevenoaks, Kent TN13 1BB. Telephone 01732 452381.
Email enquiries@jsalmon.co.uk
Design by John Curtis. Text and photographs © John Curtis
ISBN 1-902842-62-6   Printed in Italy © 2005

Title page photograph: The Lantern, Ely Cathedral
Front cover photograph: Winchester Cathedral
Back cover photograph: Oxford Cathedral